Devon Railway Station

on old picture postcards

Part Two: The Southern Railway

Andrew Swift

1. Exeter Queen Street. The LSWR station at Exeter opened in 1860, giving Exeter its second route to London. This is how it looked around 1905. The overall roof was swept away in 1933 when the station was rebuilt and renamed Exeter Central. Queen Street, unlike the GWR station at St David's, was very close to the city centre. Beyond Queen Street the line dropped down to St David's, where LSWR trains had to call before continuing onwards to Plymouth, Ilfracombe, Bude and points west. Although the old LSWR station in Exeter is still open and still busy, it is a shadow of its former self. *(Postcard published by Locomotive Publishing Company)*

Introduction

This book, like many railway books, is a nostalgic journey into the past. But it is more than that, for it shows much that was - as we are now belatedly coming to realise - needlessly destroyed in the 1960's.

Two railway companies battled it out over Devon - the Great Western (or GWR), based at Paddington, and the London & South Western (or LSWR), based at Waterloo. In the end it was the GWR that won. It got there first, picked the best routes, claimed the biggest resorts, and set out to frustrate its rival at every turn. The LSWR's route from London to Exeter was shorter than the GWR's, it is true, but the GWR had access - via Bristol - to the Midlands and the North, which the LSWR did not. Beyond Exeter, the GWR drove its line south of Dartmoor, leaving the LSWR no choice but to take its Plymouth passengers on a long and lonely journey round the north of the moor. Yet, if the LSWR was always destined to be - as far as Devon was concerned - an also-ran, it was also determined to make its mark. From its main line it sent out single-track branches to a string of seaside resorts all along the coast. It was the holiday line *par excellence*.

In 1923 the Southern Railway took over the LSWR and introduced a train, the Atlantic Coast Express, which left Waterloo daily, carrying through coaches for most of those branch-line resorts. But it all came to an end in the 1960's when the Western Region of British Railways, successors to the GWR, took over the old LSWR network in Devon and proceeded to obliterate it. At one time it seemed as though they would succeed in wiping it off the map. As it was, all the seaside branches - except the one from Exeter to Exmouth (which was more of a commuter line) - were closed. The only other branch to be spared was that from Exeter to Barnstaple. Much of the former main line from Salisbury to Exeter was singled. West of Exeter, it closed to passengers completely, except for a short section north of Plymouth.

There are signs that trains may yet return to some of the towns which lost them in the 1960's. Okehampton, where the line was kept open to serve a quarry, tops the list, but Tavistock, Sidmouth and Bideford are all candidates for a possible reinstatement of train services. It will be a long struggle before any of them do see trains again - although nothing compared to the difficulties which would face an attempt to restore services to the Ilfracombe branch.

Despite these signs of a railway renaissance, it is still sad to consider what was so wantonly thrown away. As the postcards in this book show, it was not just a transport system, it was a way of life.

Andrew Swift
June 2001

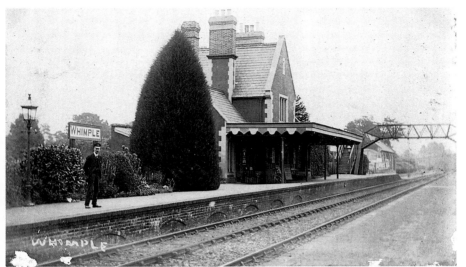

2. Whimple was a delightful station with a delightful name, made famous by the presence of Whiteway's Cider Factory, which kept the little goods yard busy for many years. The station building was designed, like most of the stations between Yeovil and Exeter, by Sir William Tite. Tite's other achievements included the Italianate stations at Southampton (1840) and Gosport (1842), and the Tudor-Gothic stations at Carlisle (1848), Perth (1848) and Windsor & Eton Riverside (1850). His most famous building, however, was the neo-classical Royal Exchange in London (1844). Whimple - minus its canopy - is still there and still open to passengers. However the singling of the line has meant the end of that wonderful footbridge. *(Chapmans of Dawlish)*

3. Sidmouth Junction. At one time this station was one of the busiest in Devon as mainline expresses connected with branch trains to Exmouth and Sidmouth. Today it is known simply as Feniton. The branches are gone, the buildings pulled down, the track singled and there is little to show that it was ever anything more than a wayside halt on a secondary line. *(Chapmans of Dawlish)*

4. Sidmouth. This red-brick, suburban-style station, hidden away at the top of a hill, was a fitting introduction to the Regency delights of this select resort where the infant Queen Victoria caught her first sight of the sea and where her father, the Duke of Kent, caught a cold and died. On this card sent from Sidmouth in June 1909 a rich array of horse-drawn transport meets a train at this select resort. *(Stengel & Co.)*

5. Sidmouth. A view of the interior of Sidmouth station from track level on a card sent from the town in 1922. Today, industrial units occupy the station site, but the main building has changed remarkably little. Although the station was 200 feet above sea level and about a mile from the town centre, Sidmouth's large retirement population should have provided the branch with a steady source of revenue. But local travel was not encouraged - right to the end, passengers to Exeter had to change at Sidmouth Junction. A through service could have saved the branch, but sadly it was not to be and the line closed in 1967. Today, however, there is a growing campaign for services to be restored. *(WH Smith)*

Honiton Railway Station

J.W.s.3054.

6. Honiton. When this card was sent from Honiton in 1906 it would have seemed inconceivable that Sir William Tite's contribution to the town's architectural heritage could be pulled down because it cost too much to maintain. Yet this impressive Jacobean-style station building, which matched the historic architecture of the lace-making town it served, has been replaced by one more suitable for a used-car lot. Maybe not such a sad loss as the Euston Arch, but still cultural vandalism of the highest order.*(J Welch, Portsmouth)*

EATON JUNCTION

7. Seaton Junction. Originally known as Colyton, this station was renamed when a four and a half mile branch was opened to Seaton in 1868. Seaton Junction has been a barometer for the fortunes of the Waterloo-Exeter line. In the late 1920's the down platform (shown here) was swept away when the tracks through the station were quadrupled. In 1966 the station closed - along with the branch to Seaton - and the line through the station reduced to a single track. *(E Pouteau, London)*

8. Axminster - a station worthy of a red carpet. Sir William Tite really went to town at Axminster. The extraordinary chimneys of this Tudor pastiche look as though they ought to be out of scale, but somehow they transform what would otherwise be a conventional - although very fine - building into something spectacular and memorable. Sadly, although the station is still open and the building still stands, the chimneys have been lopped. *(Valentines of Dundee)*

9. Axminster. A card dating from 1906 showing the station from the far side of the goods yard. At this time, and for a few years longer, just about everything that came into and went out of Axminster passed through here. The carpets which made the name of the town famous, however, were not among them. They had first been made here in 1755, but in 1835 the business was sold to a Wilton weaver who transferred it away from the town. Not until 1937 was a new carpet factory opened near Axminster station.

10. Crediton. The complex history of the five and a half mile stretch of line between Cowley Bridge Junction at Exeter and Crediton sums up all that was worst about the company rivalry which accompanied the building of the railways. Completed in 1847, it did not open for another four years, and even then arguments about ownership and gauge rumbled on for years. However, Crediton's station, which may have been designed by Brunel, is arguably the finest in Devon still in regular use. *(Woolstone Bros.)*

11. North Tawton. Round-headed windows in pointed arches break just about every rule in the book, yet the effect is certainly striking. A similar design was adopted at Bow, the next station towards Exeter, but apart from that this, ground-breaking combination of Italianate and Gothic styles seems to have had few imitators. The message on the back of the card, sent from North Tawton to Merthyr Tydfil in June 1912, reminds us that nothing was too small, or too humble, to be sent by rail in those days: *"I am sending a brace of rabbits. they are quite fresh - killed this morning."* (Chapmans of Dawlish)

12. Okehampton Military Sidings. The proximity of Dartmoor Camp and the training ranges on the moor led to these sidings being installed just south of Okehampton for troop trains. Here, on a card sent from Okehampton Camp in 1912, soldiers line up at the sidings ready for the march to the camp. In the early 1960's the sidings found a new use as the terminus of a motorail service from Surbiton.

13. The Dartmoor village of **Bridestowe** (pronounced Briddystow) was over a mile from this superbly located station. Banks of rhododendrons enhanced its charms and for added interest there was a five-mile tramroad - the Rattlebrook Peat Works Railway - leading up into the moor. The line through Bridestowe closed in 1968 and today the station is a private house. *(Chapmans of Dawlish)*

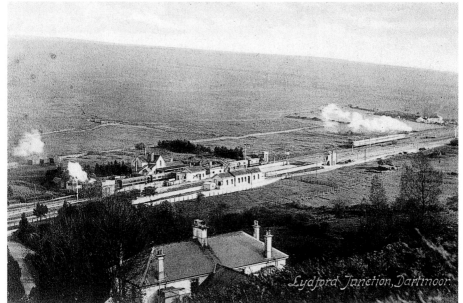

14. Lydford. Although LSWR and GWR trains met at several places in Devon, Lydford was the only one where the two companies had large stations side by side. Nothing sums up the wastefulness of nineteenth-century railway competition than this picture of two large stations in the middle of nowhere. The GWR station (nearer the camera) closed in 1962, the LSWR six years later, and today there is little to show there was ever a railway here. *(Frith)*

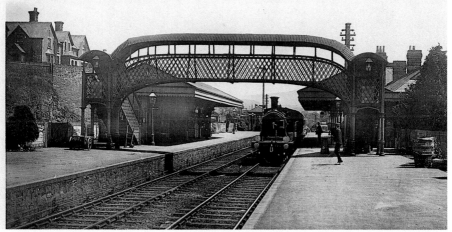

15. Tavistock. Even though the LSWR reached Lydford in 1874, its trains still had to travel over GWR metals to reach Plymouth. Not until 1890 did the nominally independent Plymouth, Devonport & South Western Junction Railway Company give the LSWR a route of its own to Plymouth. Tavistock, seen here around 1910, was the most important station on the new line. It closed in 1968 - six years after the GWR station on the other side of town - leaving Tavistock without a railway. Since then there have been many calls for its reinstatement, although the presence of buildings on the site of the old station means that a new station would have to be south of the town. *(WH Smith)*

The Station, Bere Alston.

E31994

16. Bere Alston. Beyond Tavistock came Bere Alston, from 1908 the junction for a nine and a half mile branch across the Tamar Valley to Callington. When the rest of the LSWR's Okehampton-Plymouth line closed in 1968, the Bere Alston-Plymouth section, along with the Bere Alston-Gunnislake section of the Callington branch, was reprieved because of poor road communications in the area. Although the footbridge has gone and the line singled, Bere Alston station is still open today. *(Stengel & Co.)*

BERE FERRERS 10870

17. Bere Ferrers. Also still open is the next station south, Bere Ferrers. The platform canopy has gone, but the station building - now a private house - has been carefully restored and joined by the old signalbox from Pinhoe on the Exeter-Salisbury line. In 1917 a troop train made an unscheduled stop at Bere Ferrers. A number of soldiers, thinking they had stopped for a meal break, piled out of it on the wrong side - into the path of an oncoming express. Ten were killed and many more injured. *(Chapmans of Dawlish)*

18. St. Budeaux was served by both the GWR and the LSWR. This is the LSWR station, on a card sent from Plymouth in 1907. The long covered walkway led up to the stationmaster's house. With that and the platform canopy, St Budeaux must have been an ideal place to work when it was raining - until you had to go over to the other platform. Although all the buildings - and the walkway - have gone, and the line has been singled, the LSWR station at St Budeaux, like the GWR's, is still open.

19. Ford. Though GWR and LSWR tracks converged near St Budeaux, the spirit of competition dictated that their lines should be separate for as long as possible. So the two lines parted company until meeting again just west of Plymouth's main station, North Road. Here, on the LSWR line between St Budeaux and Plymouth, is the station at Ford. It closed in 1964 when common sense finally prevailed and LSWR trains were routed onto GWR tracks at St Budeaux. The cutting has since been filled in and all trace of the station has disappeared. *(Stengel & Co.)*

20. It is hard to think of a more evocative-sounding name or a more delightfully situated station than that at **Tamerton Foliot**. Today the little trains to Gunnislake sweep through this isolated station on a wooded peninsula near the confluence of Tavy and Tamar. Its slate-hung building was different to others on the line, perhaps because it was not built until seven years after the line opened. The village it served — *"Tamar Town"* of Foliot, a twelfth-century Bishop of London — was over a mile away. The station closed in 1962. *(Chapmans of Dawlish)*

MERTON FOLIOT RY STA

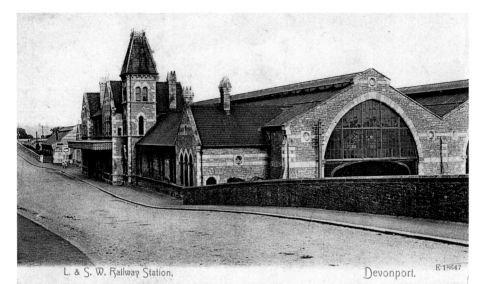

L. & S. W. Railway Station, Devonport. E 18647

21. Devonport. This impressive French Gothic style station opened in 1876 as a terminus, with the arches at this end fully glazed. From here, trains ran east to Plymouth and up the GWR line to Lydford before joining the LSWR line to Exeter. Fourteen years later, the LSWR got its own line to Lydford which entered Devonport from the west, entailing partial removal of the glazing. The overall roof and arches, damaged by bombs in World War Two, were removed in the 1950's and the station closed in 1964. The site is now occupied by a college and all trace of the station has disappeared. *(Stengel & Co.)*

22. Plymstock. This outpost of the LSWR was isolated from the rest of its system, a legacy of the competitive wrangling which characterised the development of Plymouth's rail network. To compound the confusion, Plymstock was the junction for a GWR branch to Yealmpton also isolated from the rest of its system! In this picture, GWR tracks diverge to the left while on the right the LSWR tracks continue to Turnchapel. Both lines were early victims of bus competition, and Plymstock closed to passengers in 1951.

Lapford, N. Devon.

Copyright.

23. Lapford. The Exeter-Crediton line was extended to Barnstaple in 1854. Despite only having a population of around 500, Lapford was the biggest settlement *en route*. Its station had an unusual design, with the two platforms being either side of a road bridge (out of sight to the left of this picture). Like Lifton on the GWR's Launceston branch, Lapford had an Ambrosia factory on its doorstep. This card shows the platform for Barnstaple-bound trains with the village in the background. Lapford is still open but only the platform on the other side of the bridge is now in use.

EGGESFORD, N. DEVON

24. Next stop is **Eggesford**, from where trains run down the Taw Valley towards Barnstaple. This picture captures the spirit of a bygone age so well that it is hard to believe Eggesford station is still open for business. In towns from Torrington to Tavistock, and from Bideford to Budleigh Salterton, the railway may be no more than a fading memory, but here in the quiet heart of Devon it is very much alive. This card, along with the one on the following page, was published by the then proprietor of the nearby Fox and Hounds Hotel.

EGGESFORD STATION. N. DEVON

25. Eggesford. Sitting behind the driver in one of the old-style multiple units which worked the Taw Valley line was a memorable experience and one which today's travellers can only dream of. But a journey along what is now called the *"Tarka Line,"* after Devon's most famous otter, is still a wonderful way to see a largely unknown part of Devon. For anyone interested in railways the survival of the 11 intermediate stations - including this one at Eggesford - adds further interest to the trip.

Lynton and Barnstaple Railway. Barnstaple Town Station.

26. Barnstaple Town. When the railway from Exeter was extended to Ilfracombe in 1874, a bridge was slung across the Taw and a line laid along Barnstaple's waterfront. Delightful for passengers, yet it cut Barnstaple off from the river in the same way that Dawlish was cut off from the sea. Originally trains called at a station known as Barnstaple Quay, but when the Lynton & Barnstaple Railway opened in 1898 this new station opened 250 yards to the west. The only good thing to come out of the closure of the railway to Ilfracombe in 1970 was the opening up of the waterfront at Barnstaple after almost a century. *(Pictorial Stationery Company)*

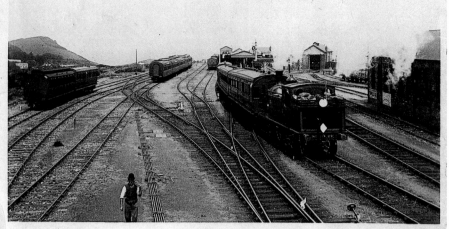

S 10793   L. & S. W. RAILWAY STATION,ILFRACOMBE.

27. A W.H. Smith *'Kingsway' series post*card of **Ilfracombe** station before the major expansion of the station in the late 1920's. Trains reached Ilfracombe in 1874 and the station was perched 225 feet above the town. *"This is the railway station here,"* wrote an unknown correspondent to her grandson in Newton Abbot in May 1915. *"Tomorrow I hope to get in one of the trains and come home to Powderham - you see the train has the engine all ready to start." (WH Smith)*

S 2500   RAILWAY STATION, ILFRACOMBE.

28. Another card showing **Ilfracombe** station with the town below. Ilfracombe station may not have been architecturally distinguished but it was well laid out, stunningly located, and with many features, such as a wooden train shed, to recommend it. It looked - and felt - like an important station, even if the only time it was stretched to capacity was on a few Saturdays each summer. Despite its inconvenient location, the railway made a vital contribution to Ilfracombe's prosperity for almost 100 years. Even today it seems inconceivable that a resort the size of Ilfracombe has no railway. *(WH Smith)*

S 6780

RAILWAY

29. Braunton station was in the middle of the village with crossing gates at either
Ilfracombe line closed in 1970 a company was founded to reopen it as a heritage lin
chairman, and for a time all looked rosy. After Sir Gerald's death in 1973, however,
be wound up. Tracklifting and demolition soon followed. Even the bridge across th
main building survived to find a new use as a shop, today it is hard to tell there w

ION, BRAUNTON.

itome of the small-town station and busy right up to the end. After the Barnstaple-
d Nabarro, who had helped the Severn Valley Railway get off the ground, was elected
ny drifted into rather dubious hands and in 1978 the Secretary of State ordered it to
nstaple was dismantled. At Braunton the station site was levelled and, although the
ilway here. *(WH Smith)*

Instow. General View.

30. A general view of **Instow** on the Torridge estuary showing the little station, opened in 1855 when the Exeter-Barnstaple line was extended to Bideford. Instow station closed in 1965, although milk and clay traffic continued to use the line until 1982. The rails were lifted in 1985 after an attempt to reopen the line as a heritage railway failed and the trackbed was turned into a cycle path. Since then, however, the old signalbox has been restored by volunteers and a section of track relaid through the station. *(TS Lake, Instow)*

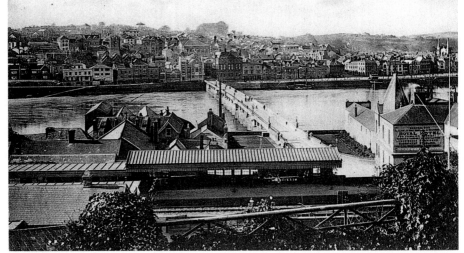

31. The railway reached **Bideford** in 1855, but the station shown here was not built until the line was extended to Torrington in 1872. It closed in 1965 but, over 35 years later, there is a museum in the signalbox, a few hundred yards of track has been relaid and the arrival of a diesel locomotive in September 2000 raises the prospect of passenger trains - albeit with a limited run - returning to Bideford. The Rail Passengers Committee for the West of England have also put reopening of the Barnstaple-Bideford line at the top of their agenda. *(GW Fluck, Bideford)*

S 3110

BIDEFORD FROM THE INSTOW ROAD.

32. The goods yard at **Bideford** marked the site of the original **1855** station. On this card, sent from Instow in 1909, goods are being transferred from horse and cart to railway wagon - or is it vice-versa? At the time, railways were the only serious form of inland transport if you wanted to go any distance. The horse ferried passengers and goods to and from the nearest station. It was an arrangement which worked well, but no competition for the point-to-point convenience of motor vehicles. *(WH Smith)*

33. The Barnstaple-Bideford line was extended to **Torrington** in 1872. The station had an idyllic location in the Torridge valley. Unfortunately, the town was over a mile away up a steep hill. Torrington, for many years the unlikely terminus for through coaches off the Atlantic Coast Express, closed to passengers in 1965 but stayed open for milk and clay traffic until 1982. The station later became a public house and the trackbed part of a cycle path.

34. Bideford Quay. For a few years there was another railway at Bideford. In 1901 a line was built along the quayside and on to Westward Ho! and Northam. Seven years later it was extended to Appledore. The Bideford, Westward Ho! and Appledore Railway had no connection with the LSWR, and through passengers had to walk or take a cab across the bridge. The line closed in 1917 when its engines and track were requisitioned for use in France. Unlike Barnstaple, which lost its waterfront to the railway, Bideford just lent its out for a few years. *(Pictorial Stationery Company)*

WESTWARD HO!

35. Westward Ho! has two claims to fame - as the only town in Britain named after a book, and the only one with an exclamation mark after its name. The resort was established in the nineteenth century and named after Charles Kingsley's novel *Westward Ho!*, part of which was set in Bideford. This postcard was sent from Westward Ho! in 1921, three years after the railway track shown on it had been lifted. *(AF Way, Westward Ho!)*

36. Westward Ho! Minstrels once entertained waiting passengers at this little station on the Atlantic coast. The nostalgic appeal of scenes such as this is almost overwhelming, yet Westward Ho! station had a life of only sixteen years. Perhaps it is the carefree confidence and faith in the future which this little line seems to embody - and which turned out to have been so misplaced - that hits us with such force.

37. In 1908 the line was extended to **Appledore**, the little port at the mouth of the Torridge. Appledore station lasted a mere nine years. Services on the Bideford, Westward Ho! and Appledore Railway were suspended on 28 March 1917. On 29 July a temporary track was laid across Bideford Bridge and the line's three tank engines puffed across it into history. Officially, services were only suspended - Bradshaw's timetable carried a blank entry until well into the twenties - but trains never returned to this remote corner of Devon, and today most people are unaware there was ever a railway here.

Lynton and Barnstaple Railway. Chelfham Station.

38. When it comes to pure unabashed nostalgia, however, the narrow-gauge Lynton & Barnstaple Railway leaves the others standing. It was open for just 37 years, from 1898 to 1935, yet it still inspires such passion that a society has been formed to restore it to its former glory. **Chelfham** station, seen here on a card from a set of 12 issued by the railway company in 1905, was purchased by the society in 1999. *(Pictorial Stationery Company)*

Lynton and Barnstaple Railway. Chelfham Station and Viaduct.

39. The station at **Chelfham** was next to this eight-arched Marland-brick viaduct, the biggest engineering work on the line. In 2000 a £450,000 restoration of the viaduct got under way. After the erection of scaffolding, the brickwork was cleaned and repaired, the parapets replaced and ballast relaid over the trackbed. All that is needed now is the track - and the trains. *(Pictorial Stationery Company)*

Lynton and Barnstaple Railway. Bratton Fleming Station.

40. Bratton Fleming. Originally known simply as Bratton, this delightfully situated station's main building was, like that at Chelfham, fairly basic, yet the whole scene exudes the magic of a bygone age. It is not just distance that lends enchantment to the view. People at the time knew that the line was somehow special. Henry Williamson, the author of *Tarka the Otter*, who lived locally, loved the Lynton & Barnstaple and featured it in many of his books. *(Pictorial Stationery Company)*

Lynton and Barnstaple Railway. Woody Bay Station.

41. Woody Bay. At close to 1,000 feet above sea level, this was once the highest station on the Southern Railway. The bay from which it took its name was three miles away down steep and narrow lanes, but a century ago an entrepreneur had plans for it. He built a pier, laid foundations for hotels and proposed to run a branch off the Lynton & Barnstaple. It all came to nothing. He went bust, the pier was swept away in a storm, and today Woody Bay is as unspoilt as it was a century ago. The station is now the headquarters of the revived Lynton & Barnstaple Heritage Railway. (Pictorial Stationery Company)

42. Blackmoor Gate. This ominously named station is today a pub and restaurant A large part of the charm of the Lynton & Barnstaple Railway is due to its stations all of which have survived. They were built by W. Jones of Lynton. Previous writers, perhaps mindful of Lynton area's promotion of itself *as "England's Switzerland,"* have commented on the chalet-like appearance of the stations at Blackmoor Gate, Woody Bay and Lynton, and their similarity to stations in Bavaria and the Austrian Tyrol. However, it is also possible to see them as part of the vernacular *cottage orné* tradition (like Blaise Hamlet near Bristol, for example) as reinterpreted by the arts-and-crafts movement. The influence - even possibly the hand - of Lutyens also seems to be hovering somewhere in the background. Given that the line's chief promoter was the wealthy and well connected Sir George Newnes, founder of the *Strand Magazine* (where Sherlock Holmes first appeared), it is perhaps not too fanciful to imagine that the design of these stations may have come, at least indirectly, from the offices of one of the most influential architects of the day.   *(Pictorial Stationery Company)*

Lynton and Barnstaple Railway. Blackm

e Station.

43. The end of the line at **Lynton**. The story of how the railway came to Lynton is extraordinary - and possibly unique. In the 1890's, with Britain's railway network almost complete, the GWR, eager to expand into new areas, turned its attention to the twin villages of Lynton and Lynmouth. The well-heeled residents of the area were up in arms. A railway meant day-trippers, and an end to the tranquility they had come to enjoy. They decided on a unique plan of action. They would build their own railway - but build it so that nobody would want to use it. They decided it would be narrow gauge, with less than two feet between the rails. When it opened in 1898 it took an hour and forty minutes to travel to the junction with the main line at Barnstaple, 19 and a half miles away. As if that was not enough, the station at Lynton was 250 feet above the town. Not surprisingly it was a financial disaster, yet for its promoters it was a resounding success. Although the railway was open for a mere 37 years, they succeeded in preserving the unique character of their corner of North Devon. *(Montague Cooper)*

Railway Station.

Lynton and Barnstaple Railway. Lynton and Lynmouth Station.

44. In 1923 the Lynton & Barnstaple was taken over by the Southern Railway. Twelve years later, despite many protests, the directors at faraway Waterloo decided that it had to close. The last train pulled out of **Lynton**, with the town band playing *Auld Lang Syne*, on Sunday 29 September 1935. It was - and is - sadly missed. But, with a society now dedicated to its restoration, the words of the wreath placed on the buffer stops at Barnstaple Town station the morning after it closed - *"Perchance it is not dead but sleepeth"* - may yet prove prophetic. *(Pictorial Stationery Company)*

TOPSHAM STATION

45. From a railway awakening from a 70-year torpor to one that is very much awake. The old port of **Topsham** on the Exe estuary, with its Dutch-style houses, is served by this splendid station. The signalbox which once controlled the crossing gates in the distance closed in 1988 when its functions were transferred to a distant power box and it became an office. This card was sent from Topsham, in September 1909. *(Osborne, Topsham)*

46. Like the station buildings on the main line between Exeter and Axminster, **Topsham**'s was built by Sir William Tite. Today it is no longer used by the railway. Its canopy has gone, its brick rendered and it is cut off from the platform by a fence - but at least it is still there. This card was posted from the town in April 1910, and shows a typically busy scene. Although Topsham station is busier than ever, a once-busy goods branch down to the wharf on the Exe closed in 1957. *(Hopewell, Topsham)*

47. Lympstone. The run from Exeter St David's down along the Exe to Dawlish Warren is justly celebrated, but how many know the little line to Exmouth which slips down the opposite bank of the estuary? Opened in 1861 and still busy with commuter traffic, it is the only one of the LSWR's seaside branches in Devon to have survived the devastation which in just four years (1966-70) saw all the others disappear. On this card, an Exmouth-bound train sweeps past a riverside cottage near the old fishing village of Lympstone. *(Chapmans of Dawlish)*

48. Perched on the edge of the Exe estuary is this station at **Woodbury Road**, wit its slate-hung buildings. It opened in 1861 and was renamed Exton in 1958. He an Exmouth-bound train pulls into the well-staffed but poorly-patronised static on a postcard postmarked May 1916. Back then, low wages - with railwayme earning an average of 25/- a week - meant that what seems to us like profliga overstaffing was less of a problem. *(Chapmans of Dawlish)*

WOODBURY ROAD RY STATION

GENTLEMEN

PEARS

WEAR
FRISBY
BOOT

N 13263

Railway Station, Exmouth.

49. Exmouth was already an established resort by the time a branch from Exeter reached it in 1861. So heavy was traffic on the branch early last century that the section from Exeter to Topsham was doubled, and another line to Exmouth was opened from Sidmouth Junction. In 1924, shortly after the Southern Railway took over, they built this splendid new Queen Anne style terminus which was demolished in the 1970's and replaced by a bus stop. Any further comment seems superfluous. *(WH Smith)*

Littleham Station, Exmouth.

50. Littleham. Exmouth got its second railway in 1903 when the line from Sidmouth Junction to Budleigh Salterton was extended. The only station between Budleigh Salterton and Exmouth was Littleham, on the outskirts of Exmouth. Here the station is seen on a card posted from Exmouth in 1919. The line through Littleham closed in 1967, and today a road runs through the site of the station, with the stationmaster's house the only sign that there was ever a station there.

51. Ottery St. Mary. *"Just a pc for your collection"* is the only message on this card sent from Ottery St Mary in 1906. A well-dressed crowd waits on the platform as a train pulls in. Although Ottery St Mary had a daily service to London, most branch trains only went as far as Sidmouth Junction, with passengers having to change for Exeter. This, especially after buses appeared on the scene, discouraged local travel and helped the case of those who wanted to close the line. The last trains ran on 6 March 1967 and the station building became a youth centre. *(RT Slee, Ottery St Mary)*

52. Ashbury. This isolated station between Okehampton and Halwill Junction opened in 1879, and is seen here on a card sent from Pilton on 12 December 1907. Although many holidaymakers must have passed through Ashbury over the years, *en route* to Bude or Padstow, it was far from any tourist trail. It closed, hardly changed from the day it opened, along with the entire ex-LSWR network west of Okehampton, in 1966.

Halwill Station

53. Halwill. In 1879 the LSWR opened this wayside station on the Okehampton-Holsworthy branch and called it Beaworthy. Slowly the network expanded and eventually you could catch a train from Beaworthy (renamed Halwill Junction in 1887) to the four points of the compass - west to Bude, east to Okehampton, south to Launceston and north to Torrington. Then, in less than two years (1965-1966) it was all swept away. Today all there is to indicate there was once a railway here is a road on a housing estate called Beeching Close.

54. Tower Hill. It is hard to think of a greater contrast between this outpost of the LSWR and the London underground station with which it shared its name. It opened in 1886 when the Halwill to Launceston line opened and closed 80 years later in 1966. Sadly, the station buildings were later demolished — apparently by a builder who had been brought in to tidy up the site and misunderstood his instructions. *(RAP Co Ltd, London)*